Who Will Help Jack Off the Horse?

written by Bimisi Tayanita

illustrated by Sumguyen Bangladesh

created by Matt Williams, literary alchemist

Copyright ©2020 Reach Around Books, LLC.
PO BOX 910555 Saint George UT 84791

ISBN 978-1-946178-07-7   First printing   Printed with love, in China.

"Who Will Help Jack Off the Horse?" is the first of five books that make up Season Two.

www.ReachAroundBooks.com

I am Morse.
Morse of course.

I would not do it here or there.
I would not do it anywhere.

All that I can say is "WOW!"

I would not help Jack off a cow.

Not here.
Not there.
Not then.
Not now...

I would not help Jack off a cow.

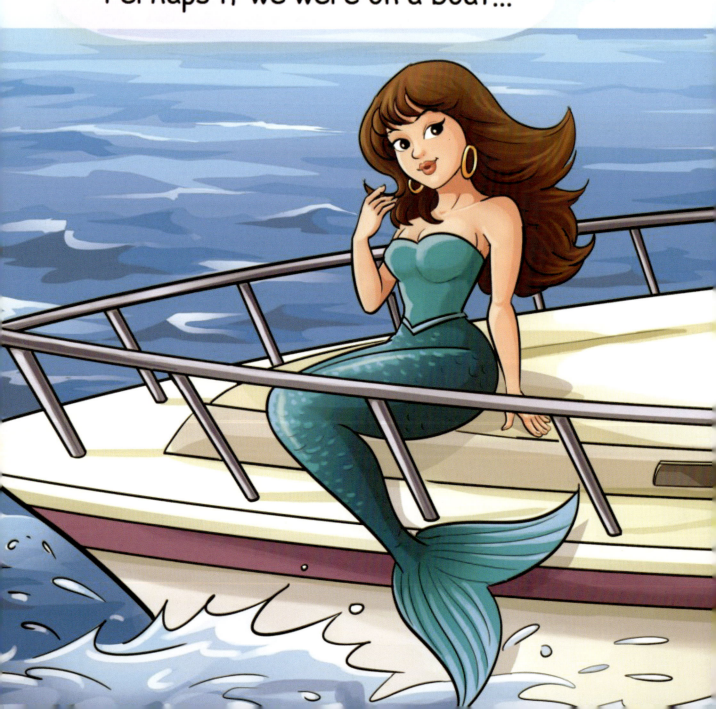

Perhaps if we were on a boat...

If I find myself afloat
  with you and Jack aloft a goat
  I will dive into the sea...

  and that's the last you'll see of me.

I would not help Jack off the horse.
I would not do it Morse of course.

I would not help Jack off a cow.
Not in the past.
Not in the now.

You say you like it in the sea?
In the sea you say to me?

Help Jack off a whale today?

For years to come
they'll tell the tale...